TELFORD
THEN & NOW
IN COLOUR

DAVID TRUMPER

The
History
Press

To my wife Wendy for all her help and encouragement over the past forty-four years.

First published in 2013

The History Press
The Mill, Brimscombe Port
Stroud, Gloucestershire, GL5 2QG
www.thehistorypress.co.uk

© David Trumper, 2013

The right of David Trumper to be identified as the Author
of this work has been asserted in accordance with the
Copyrights, Designs and Patents Act 1988.

British Library Cataloguing in Publication Data.
A catalogue record for this book is available from the British Library.

ISBN 978 0 7524 7742 8

Typesetting and origination by The History Press
Printed in India.

CONTENTS

ACKNOWLEDGEMENTS

I gratefully acknowledge the past publications of the area listed in the bibliography, which I have used when writing the captions for the photographs. I would also like to thank the staff at the Shropshire Records and Research Centre for all their help in my researches. I would like to acknowledge the help I have received from articles written in the *Shropshire Star* by their Nostalgia Editor Toby Neal and the informative replies by *Star* readers. Both have done a great deal in recent years to reveal the county's interesting past. My thanks go to Jim Ball and Bill Parton and a number of local people I met during my visits to Telford, who helped me find the right locations. My thanks also go to my wife Wendy, who accompanied me on my trips to take the modern views and also reviewed the text.

BIBLIOGRAPHY

Baugh, G.C., ed., *The Victoria History of Shropshire*, Vol. XI (OUP, 1985)

Brown, F. and Pollard, T.W., *Public Houses of Wellington from 1800* (Wellington Civic Society, 1996)

Eaton, A.G., *Madeley in Old Picture Postcards* (Zaltbommel/Netherlands, 1990)

Evans, G., *Wellington: A Portrait in Old Photographs and Picture Postcards* (S.B. Publications, 1990)

Evans, G. and Briscoe, R., *Telford: A Pictorial History* (Phillimore, 1995)

Gilder, T., *Hadley in Old Picture Postcards* (Zaltbommel/Netherlands, 1998)

Kelly's Directory of Shropshire, various dates

Oakengates in the words of Oakengates People (Telford Community Arts, 1987)

The Shrewsbury Chronicle, various issues

Trinder, B., *The Industrial Revolution in Shropshire* (Phillimore, 1981)

Trinder, B., *The Industrial Archaeology of Shropshire* (Phillimore, 1996)

INTRODUCTION

In 1968 the government decided to enlarge the area of a new town that had been designated Dawley New Town in 1963. The new town was to be called Telford and was 10 miles from north to south and 3 miles across at its widest point. The new town was named after Scotsman Thomas Telford, who became the Surveyor of Public Works for the county and made Shropshire his adopted home. He was known as the 'Father of Civil Engineering' and his influence on the county and beyond can still be seen today.

The architects and planners of the new town were faced with a daunting task as the area they had been given was not an empty canvas but a range of contrasting landscapes made up of large settlements, villages and hamlets, agricultural land and large areas of disused industrial sites. The Industrial Revolution that had started over 200 years before had come and gone, leaving a legacy of decay. There were over 5,000 acres of derelict wasteland containing spoil heaps and pit mounds, over 2,000 uncapped mine shafts, and stagnant pools and abandoned forges, furnaces and other industrial buildings.

Another problem for the planners was how to pacify the inhabitants of the five main townships of Wellington, Oakengates, Dawley, Madeley and Ironbridge, who were fiercely independent and mindful of their rights. The Telford Development Corporation wisely did not try to destroy the individuality of these townships, but left them as district centres, linking them together with an amazing network of bypasses and roads. The road system with all its traffic islands can be quite confusing, as Ken Dodd found out when he arrived forty-five minutes late for the opening of Dawley High Street in September 1980, suffering from what he called 'a severe case of the Telford round-a-bouts.'

Once the road network was in place, the areas in between were filled in with housing estates, schools and other amenities. Large industrial estates followed, as well as a spacious town centre with large departmental stores and shops, offices, civic buildings, an extensive town park and many other recreational facilities for a fast-growing population.

All the old photographs in this book were taken between 1890 and 1970. The development of the new town and the vast changes that took place has made it impossible in some cases to take a modern photograph from the same vantage point. In the Ironbridge Gorge in particular, growth of trees and bushes along the steep slopes of the river have made it difficult to obtain the same view. The modern photographs, taken during the spring and summer of 2012, have therefore been taken from the best possible position.

ADMASTON

THE FOUR TURNINGS, Admaston, *c.*1920. It is thought that the name of the village is derived from 'Edmund's Homestead'. The house on the left, for obvious reasons, is called The Gables, while the house on the other corner is the Manor House. In this period the Manor House was the home of William Morgan, perhaps the man standing at the gate. At this crossroads, the road to the left leads to Bratton; Hadley lies straight ahead and Wellington is to the right.

UNTIL THE MIDDLE of the twentieth century this was a quiet little village on the outskirts of Wellington, but with the advent of Telford New Town it saw large-scale housing projects developed. This scene has changed little, save that the road has now been properly surfaced and yellow lines put on the corners to stop people parking near the junction. A pavement has also been provided and the foliage cut back to give a better view of both properties.

MARKET SQUARE, WELLINGTON

THE MARKET SQUARE, Wellington, looking towards Church Street, *c.*1950. The market moved to this site from The Green, to the north of All Saints' church, in 1244. It once included Bell Street, Duke Street and Crown Street, but these were eventually built over. On the left, with its grand entrance, is the Wrekin Hotel. In the last quarter of the nineteenth century Thomas Taylor, who also had a brewery in Wrekin Street, owned the Wrekin Hotel. In the twentieth century it became a commercial hotel run by Mabel Chinock and later a temperance hotel.

THE GROUND FLOOR was gradually taken over by shops. Stead and Simpson sold shoes and were there from the start of the twentieth century. After the hotel closed, the upper floors were converted into office space. Today, Market Square has been paved over and pedestrianized, with traffic being diverted down Market Street. Benches have also been provided for weary shoppers, and a smart 'Community Clock'.

CHURCH STREET, WELLINGTON

CHURCH STREET, WELLINGTON, *c.*1905. The man on the right is walking past the wall of the parish church, All Saints'. On the left is the drapers' shop belonging to J.L. and E.T. Morgan and above them is the premises of James Smith & Son, who were licensed to sell wines and spirits. The tall building is Lloyds Bank and on the corner is the ironmonger's belonging to S. Corbett & Son, who were also engineers, agricultural implement makers and grinding mill

manufacturers. The building to the right is the post office. At this period it was open on weekdays from 7 a.m. until 9 p.m. and on Sundays, Good Friday and Christmas Day from 8 a.m. to 10 a.m. for telegraph business only.

PARKED CARS NOW dominate the scene. The drapers' shop has become the Tender Fried Chicken and has changed very little, but the top storey of James Smith & Son has been rebuilt. It is still a public house, today called The Bacchus Inn. The building next door is the same but the bank and ironmonger's have been rebuilt. The post office has closed and the building has been split into smaller units.

NEW STREET, WELLINGTON

NEW STREET, WELLINGTON, *c*.1950. This photograph was taken looking towards the Market Square. William Bentley was landlord of the Duke of Wellington, on the right, from 1870 until 1905. He sported a 12in beard and kept a rack of Broseley pipes behind the bar for the use of his customers. At the time of the 1896 census of inns it had five rooms downstairs and seven upstairs, as well as stabling for nine horses. On the left is Sidoli's café, which was once an inn known as The Shakespeare. In the nineteenth century it opened early in the morning and served

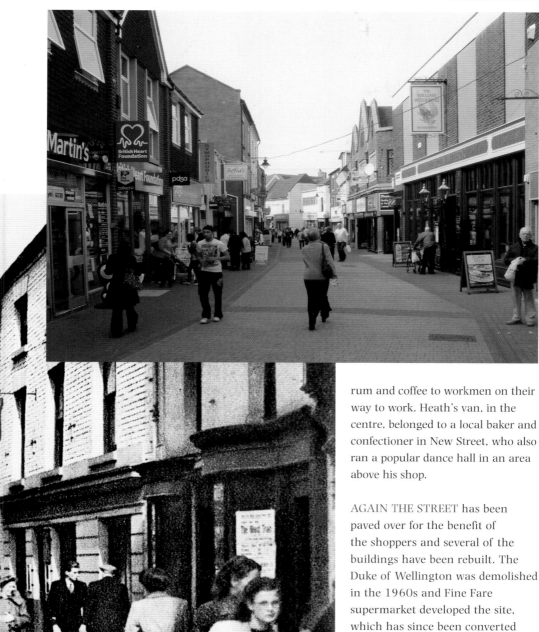

rum and coffee to workmen on their way to work. Heath's van, in the centre, belonged to a local baker and confectioner in New Street, who also ran a popular dance hall in an area above his shop.

AGAIN THE STREET has been paved over for the benefit of the shoppers and several of the buildings have been rebuilt. The Duke of Wellington was demolished in the 1960s and Fine Fare supermarket developed the site, which has since been converted back to a Wetherspoon's inn called The William Withering. Sidoli's café is now Sofia's restaurant and coffee house.

THE CATTLE MARKET, WELLINGTON

THE CATTLE MARKET, Wellington, *c.*1910. Animals have been sold at fairs in Wellington since 1244. By 1825 cattle fairs were held on land to the north of All Saints' church, while the horse fairs were held at the top of New Street. By 1855 the sale of cattle had moved to a site south-east of the railway station, where it stayed until the cattle plague of 1866. The following year a new market was opened in Bridge Street, next to the railway station, and by 1879 sales of livestock were held there every Monday.

THE MARKET OCCUPIED the site for over 100 years until it was redeveloped into a Morrisons supermarket. New housing has been built in the area and a large traffic island is visible behind the cars. The building just above the cattle sheds on the old view, whose chimneys are visible above the car wash on the new view, was until 2012 the office for registering births, deaths and marriages.

MILL BANK, WELLINGTON

MILL BANK, WELLINGTON, *c.*1910. Two cars approach the junction of the A5 and the A442 on what is now an extremely busy crossroads. As more vehicles began to use the roads a traffic island was introduced, which in turn was replaced by traffic lights. In 1896 the Cock Hotel was owned and occupied by Mrs Martha Freeman. The property contained eight rooms on the ground floor and eleven upstairs. The timber-framed house across the road is the Swan Hotel, while the double-fronted house next door was the Anchor until it was closed in 1916.

BOTH THE COCK and the Swan survive, although the old Swan, which was a Grade II listed building, was demolished in 1959 and a new one was built further back from the road and at an angle. In March 1996 the Cock became Wellington's first Real Ale public house selling a variety of brews in a bar called 'The Old

Wrekin Tap'. The Anchor, which was only a small inn with just six rooms and stabling for one horse, was converted into a private house. It was demolished, along with the cottages to the side, for car parking space soon after the new Swan was built.

THE SQUARE, HADLEY

THE SQUARE, HADLEY, *c.*1905. The Square was
at the junction of several roads radiating to other
settlements in the area. Richard Brittain was a family
grocer and provisions merchant; the shop was later
a chemist's run by Bates and Hunt before it was
demolished. The shop, on the corner of Castle Street
and Church Street, belonged to Robert Heenan, a
grocer and baker; it was later taken over by Melias.
The house in the centre of Castle Street belonged to
Henry Woodfin, a boot repairer.

MANY PROPERTIES HAVE now been demolished and
the roads realigned, making life easier for motorists.
The only building remaining from the old view is the
white building in Castle Street, which belonged to
Henry Woodfin. He had a workshop in a lean-to shed
at the rear of the house, where for many years Lenny
Baker did the shoe and boot repairs.

THE SQUARE, HADLEY

THE SQUARE, HADLEY, *c.*1905. Mr Shutt the pork butcher advertised home-cured hams and bacon and fresh pies and sausages that were made daily. Primitive Methodism reached Hadley in about 1838. A chapel was erected on the corner of Gladstone Street and the Square in 1841 and was rebuilt in a much grander scale in 1879. The new chapel, which saddled the congregation with a huge debt, never thrived and by 1910 attendances were very poor. By the 1920s the building was found to be unsafe and services were moved into the schoolroom. In 1933, with a congregation of just nine, the chapel closed and was sold.

THE SPIRE WAS removed and the building was
converted into a cinema called the Regal that ran from
1934 to 1957. It was then developed into a tyre depot
that also sold batteries and other motor parts, before
it was demolished and new housing built on the site.
Gladstone Street, to the side, has also seen a great deal
of redevelopment in recent years.

COALPORT BRIDGE, HADLEY

THE COALPORT BRIDGE, Hadley, 30 July 1966. The bridge is close to where Castle Street ends and Trench Lock begins. It once carried goods and passenger traffic down a branch line from Wellington to Coalport, running from 1861 until its closure by Dr Beeching in September 1964. Other stations on the line included Oakengates, Malinslee, Dawley and Madeley Market. The line was built along sections of the Shropshire Canal that, by the mid-nineteenth century, had fallen into disrepair.

ON A TIGHT bend in the road, this area was the scene of many crashes and the bridge was demolished shortly after the old photograph was taken in April 1967. Just under the bridge (on the left, behind the wall and railings) used to be the site of Sankey's cricket pitch, but the site is now occupied by the new Greenhous' Garage and showrooms. The houses on the right are still standing and the area has been landscaped.

TRENCH

TRENCH, *c.*1935. In the *Kelly's Directory* for 1921 this short description was given: 'The Trench is a straggling hamlet about 1.5 miles in length, principally in the township of Wrockwardine Wood, from which place it is nearly a mile distant, and has a station called "Trench Crossing" on the London and North West railway. Here is a Primitive Methodist chapel built in 1866. A volunteer fire brigade was organised in 1916.'

BOTH VIEWS WERE taken opposite the New Inn looking towards Hadley and show that little has changed in the past seventy years. The two pairs of semi-detached houses on the right are Holly and Ivy Villas and Jesmond and Gordeston Villas. Again, most of the properties have had their walls and hedges removed to allow cars to park on their fronts.

TRENCH CROSSING STATION

TRENCH CROSSING STATION, *c.*1920. This line, which ran between Wellington and Stafford, was opened by the Shropshire Union Railway on 1 June 1849. The line was 18.5 miles long and had other stations in Shropshire at Hadley, Donnington and Newport. The line was taken over by the London & North Western Railway in 1922 before becoming part of the London, Midland & Scottish Railway in 1923. The stationmaster's house is on the far left while the little cabin on the right is the ladies' waiting room. The building in the centre is the ticket office and gentlemen's waiting room.

THE STATION CLOSED to passengers on 7 September 1964 and the line to freight traffic on 1 August 1966. Most of the buildings were demolished but the stationmaster's house, which was later occupied by the crossing keeper, still survives. The house behind the waiting room is still there, as is part of the track. The single line runs between Wellington and the Central Ordnance Depot at Donnington and is rarely used.

DONNINGTON
WOOD MILL

DONNINGTON WOOD MILL, *c.*1920. Although called Donnington Wood Mill, the building was erected on the north side of the Shrewsbury Canal, just visible on the left, at Wrockwardine Wood. The tall building was erected in 1891, although the origins of the mill date back

to 1818. In that year John Boycott, John Duncombie and John Horton went into partnership and erected a steam flour mill, granary and bakery. Richard Ogle was taken into the partnership, but by 1871 John Bullock, who had started work at the mill as a young clerk, had become the sole owner. The business continued until 1943 and the building was known locally as Bullock's Mill.

THE CANAL HAS been filled in and the mill converted into apartments, which belong to the Beth Johnson Housing Association in partnership with Wrockwardine Wood and Trench Parish Councils. A small housing estate surrounds the mill on the right and a single-storey building has been built in front, which is an unmanned police office. The date of 1891 is still visible on the eave of the tall building.

THE SUTHERLAND ARMS, MUXTON

THE SUTHERLAND ARMS, Muxton, 31 December 1963. This was the last New Year's Eve that the old inn would see, as demolition was imminent. In the 1901 survey it was owned by the Duke of Sutherland and managed by Urian Cowper Pearce, who was also a farmer. On 11 October 1898, Mr Pearce was prosecuted for 'selling intoxicating liquor to drunken persons' and fined £2 plus 17s 6d costs. The inn was known locally as Smokey Joe's.

THE SUTHERLAND ARMS stands on the Wellington Road with the photographer looking towards Lilleshall. The space left by the demolition of the old inn is used as a car park for the new Sutherland Arms built at the rear. The new inn can be seen clearly on the old photograph but is hidden by trees on the new view – only the eaves are visible between the branches. On land just beyond the inn is Breton Park Homes, a neatly laid out area of static homes for holidays and retirement.

THE POST OFFICE, WROCKWARDINE WOOD

THE POST OFFICE, Wrockwardine Wood, *c.*1900. William Harper was sub-post master from the 1880s until the 1920s. In 1891 his shop was listed as a post office, money-order office, savings bank and an annuity and insurance office. The post office received letters sorted at Wellington that arrived by foot each weekday morning at 8 a.m., with letters dispatched from there at 5.05 p.m. Mr Harper hired out traps and waggonettes from there and he was also a grocer and baker. Note the post office delivery cart to the left of the window.

BEFORE THE BUILDINGS were demolished to leave this more open view, they became part of the Beehive Bakery. The photographer is standing outside the Red Lion Inn on New Road looking towards the junction of Lincoln Road on the right. The wooded area to the rear is known as Cockshutt Piece, an area used in former times to catch wild birds by hanging nets across an open space of land in the wood.

WROCKWARDINE WOOD

WROCKWARDINE WOOD, *c*.1913. Harry Walter Poole occupied this shop on the corner of Middle Road from about 1898 until 1935. He was listed as a provisions merchant, grocer, tea dealer, butcher and a beer retailer, selling Cheshire's Pale Ales. Although the shop seemed

to cater for most things, there were still another four grocery shops in the village and another eight inns or beer retailers listed! The photograph was taken for a publicity postcard by H. Lord of Wolverhampton and shows Mr Poole outside his establishment.

THIS IS THE junction of Lincoln Road and Middle Road on the right. Mr Poole's shop has been demolished and modern housing built on the site. The only indication that this is the site of the store is the slight gradient on Middle Road as it runs down towards New Road.

CROSSROADS, ST GEORGE'S

THE CROSSROADS, ST George's, 29 September 1967. The *Shropshire Star* headline read: 'Stop: There's a Crisis at the Crossroads!', and reported the measures taken to improve one of Telford's notorious accident black spots. The council's attention was drawn to the new halt signs that had been erected just 4½ yards from the junction, with no advance warning and no electricity connected to illuminate the signs at night. One shopkeeper commented that cars travelling at speed were on top of the junction before they realised it was there. Strangers involved in accidents often claimed they had not seen the halt sign.

BOTH VIEWS ARE taken from West Street looking towards Church Street, with Gower Street on the left and Stafford Street on the right. Both Gower Street and Stafford Street were named after aristocratic families who owned land in the area. After years of petitions and debate, the traffic problem was finally resolved with the demolition of the building on the left behind the two ladies and the removal of the Oakengates and District Co-op shop on the opposite corner. Their removal opened up the view and allowed a mini island to be installed that permitted traffic to flow freely.

THE CHURCH
OF ST GEORGE

THE CHURCH OF St George, *c.*1910. A chapel of ease was erected in Pains Lane in 1806 on
land donated by the Marquess of Stafford. It was paid for by the Lilleshall Co. and from money
left in the will of Isaac Hawkins Browne, a local landowner. It was licensed for baptisms
and burials in 1806 and marriages in 1837. The old building was poorly built, and when

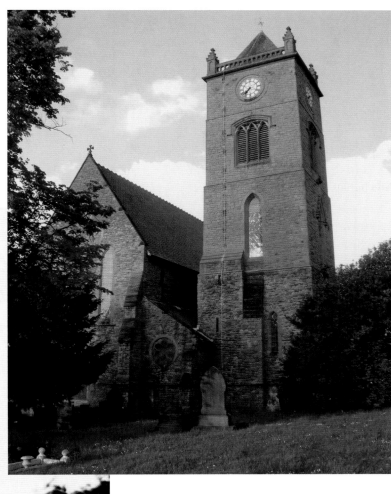

St George's was made into a separate parish the authorities decided to build a new church on the same site. This church was designed by G.E. Street and consecrated in 1862 at a cost of £4,000.

THE CHURCH HAS a tunnel-vaulted chancel, a four-bayed nave, a vestry and a south porch. It was built out of brick with a grey and red stone dressing. The original idea by Street was to give the church a tower and stone spire but Bertram Butler, who redesigned the tower, gave it a pyramid roof instead. The tower was completed in 1929, the same year that a set of mechanically operated bells known as a carillon was added.

THE GREEN, OAKENGATES

THE GREEN, OAKENGATES, *c.*1970. This is a view across The Green to Market Street, taken from under the railway bridge. On the left is the Coffee Palace, built in 1895. It acted as a Temperance Hall until 1913 and was also the centre for art and science classes until the Walker Technical College was opened in 1927. Classes took place on five nights of the week and on Saturdays courses for teachers and pupil-teachers were held. The council also used the Palace for a short time as an employment exchange and a place to register births, deaths and marriages. Duncan Ball's hardware shop is on the ground floor; he also owned the footwear shop to the left.

THE ROAD ON the left is New Street. Its entrance was widened in around 1946 when two buildings were demolished leaving The Green Inn on the corner. The inn was licensed to sell Wrekin Ales. Throughout the late nineteenth and early twentieth centuries it had a quick turnover of landlords. The Coffee Palace was demolished by the New Town Corporation 'to make way for improvement'. A similar fate was suffered by the building on the right at the junction of Lion Street, which housed George Mason's grocery shop. The Green Inn has also closed and is now a hair and beauty centre.

STATION YARD, LION STREET, OAKENGATES

STATION YARD, LION STREET, Oakengates, 4 March 1966. Railways played a vital role in local industry and many firms had siding by their factories, linked to the main lines. The GWR goods yard would have been a hive of activity at the beginning of the twentieth century, but by the time

this photograph was taken local industry was dying out. The large building in the centre is the GWR goods shed. The white building at the bottom of the street is the Brown Lion, while in the top left-hand corner, in the distance behind the goods shed, is the Walker Technical College.

THE NEGLECTED ROAD on the old view has been resurfaced and a pavement and parking bay have been put in on the right. New buildings have been erected on part of the site, which has also been landscaped, but some work is still ongoing. The Brown Lion has closed and is now a pizza parlour.

STATION HILL

OAKENGATES STATION AND the Grosvenor Cinema, Market Street, *c.*1930. In 1857 the Coalport Branch Railway, which later became the LNWR, was able to purchase the old Shropshire Canal to build their line from Hadley Junction to Coalport. It was opened to freight in 1860 and for passengers a year later. This station closed to passengers in 1952 and for goods in 1964. Other stations on the line were at Malinslee and Madeley. The cinema was opened in 1923, and was built by casual labour, the men apparently having to provide their own tools. The cinema was always a popular rendezvous, and in 1932 seats were priced at 2*d*, 3*d* and 6*d*. The picture house closed in 1967 and was demolished in 1975 to make way for the new ring road.

THE CAR IS driving up Station Hill, which takes its name from the old railway station. It was Oakengates' second station. The main one on Station Road was opened in 1849 on what was the Shrewsbury to Birmingham Railway. On the right is Cockshutt Road, which led round to The Nabb. The bridge carries the A442 from Horton Wood in north Telford through to Brookside in the south and is known as the Queensway. The buildings through the bridge are at the top of Market Street.

THE SEVEN STARS, KETLEY

THE SEVEN STARS, Ketley, 22 December 1964. A sad day for the people of Ketley as the bulldozer moves in and demolishes the old inn just three days before Christmas. The inn was built in about 1576 as a posting station and was reputed to be the oldest coaching inn on the London to Holyhead Road. Behind the brick façade was a timber-framed structure with wattle and daub walls and sloping floors. The famous highwayman Dick Turpin is said to have lodged there. Many of the landlords have heard the ghostly noises of a young woman who was murdered there.

IT WAS AT the old inn that John Parton founded a sick club for local miners and ironworkers. For a small weekly contribution the men were assured a weekly payment when they fell ill, and a large lump sum for the family when they died. Before the old inn was demolished a new inn was built at the rear. Part of the roof can be seen on the left of the old view. It was known as the Elephant and Castle but has since become the Blue Elephant, serving Indian cuisine.

GREENHOUS' GARAGE, HOLYHEAD ROAD

GREENHOUS' GARAGE, HOLYHEAD Road, *c.*1942. Vincent Greenhous left the family business in Bishop's Castle in 1913 when he moved to Shrewsbury and set up his own motor business in Meadow Place. He was a shrewd businessman and soon his business was expanding throughout

Shropshire and beyond. He acquired this business from Irving Brothers, who opened the garage on Potter's Bank on the old A5 in the 1920s, and the site has been redeveloped many times over the years.

ON 27 AUGUST 2000, Greenhous showed his commitment to Telford by opening a state-of-the-art garage and showrooms at Trench Lock in Hadley. This garage has since been taken over by Citroen. The bungalows on each side have been demolished as the garage and showrooms have been extended but the main section looks very similar to the building on the old photograph. Behind the complex, at the bottom of a very steep bank, lies the hamlet of Beveley.

HOLYHEAD ROAD

THE GREYHOUND, HOLYHEAD Road, 1 May 1973. The Greyhound stood on the junction of this crossroads on the old London to Holyhead Road from about 1800. The photographer is looking towards Wellington, with Maddock's works and Oakengates town centre to the right and Ketley Bank to the left. The buildings on the junction opposite belong to the Greyhound Garage. At the beginning of the nineteenth century the inn was owned by the Union Brewery & Co. of Wellington. Its customers were mainly ironworkers and miners with some passing trade.

THE MODERN VIEW is taken from a busy traffic island known as the Greyhound Interchange, which links the Holyhead Road with the Queensway. In 1973 a lorry embedded itself into the side of the inn, narrowly missing customers in a packed bar. The damage was severe and the inn did not reopen until June 1974, eighteen months after the accident. It closed around the mid-1990s and is now a Domino's pizza parlour.

TELFORD CENTRAL
RAILWAY STATION

TELFORD CENTRAL RAILWAY Station, 10 August 1985. With just nine months before the formal opening, the two main platforms are down, but the car park, ticket office, waiting rooms and other services have still to be erected. The two 30-metre platforms were long enough for intercity trains. Lord Murray of Telford and Epping formally opened the station – built jointly by British Rail and the Telford Development Corporation – on 12 May 1986. Lord Murray was born in Hadley in 1922 and was brought up in the area. As Len Murray, he was the highly respected General Secretary of the TUC for many years.

THIS STATION WAS built at Hollinswood, within easy walking distance of the new town centre. The covered walkway connecting the platforms to the main shopping area can be seen at the top of the view. Trees and bushes hide a great deal of the infrastructure but a waiting area can be seen on the left while part of the main station is on the right. Due to the increase of use, the car park has been greatly extended and the main station building is now being updated. The road leading down to the station was named Euston Way.

DAWLEY BANK

DAWLEY BANK, 27 October 1966. The families that lived in these cottages had been moved out almost a year before the demolition men moved in and reduced them to a pile of rubble. A number of the families were re-housed close by in smart new council flats in Powis Place. Many, however, still made a pilgrimage back to their old homes on washing day to hang out their washing. One resident explained to the *Shropshire Star*:'We are not supposed to hang out our washing outside the flats. There are special drying cabinets, which are quite adequate. But when there is a nice day quite a few of us go over and use the old lines at the cottages.'

THE OPEN ASPECT gives a good view of the old Baptist church. The first church was built on this site in 1846 but replaced in 1860 as the congregation grew. It was built out of blue brick with a yellow and red brick dressing. It had an elaborate gable with ball-shaped finials and could seat 600. It fell victim to the demolition gangs in 2000 and was replaced with this modern multi-purpose building. The cottages on the right remain; one is now used as Cecil Walker's grocery shop and post office.

MARKET HALL, DAWLEY

THE MARKET HALL, Dawley, *c*.1900. Early in the nineteenth century the township of Dawley moved from around the old parish church to this area. The Market Hall was erected in 1867 and was built out of red brick with an ornamental frontage and vaults underneath. The frontage was once topped by a turret containing a bell and a clock presented by Lt-Col William Kenyon Slaney who, in a guide for 1882, was described as 'lord of the manor'. Down Chapel Street at the rear of the hall was a potato market.

AFTER THE BUILDING of the Dawley Green Way, traffic no longer traversed this street. In September 1980, therefore, a new pedestrianized High Street was opened by comedian Ken Dodd, who was performing at Oakengates Town Hall at the time. In an attempt to bring more trade into the centre, a new one-way system with parking bays was introduced in 2011. All the buildings remain, although the roof of the market has been replaced and the frontage greatly altered.

HIGH STREET, DAWLEY

HIGH STREET, DAWLEY, *c.*1925. The market hall is on the left and the building straight ahead is the Elephant and Castle public house. On the left is Phillip's Stores, who had shops in towns all around the county. They were listed as grocers and tea dealers. The men and boys are standing outside Horace Smith's barber's; he later moved his business into Burton Street. The shop with the large awning belonged to Benjamin Preece & Son, a shoemaker,

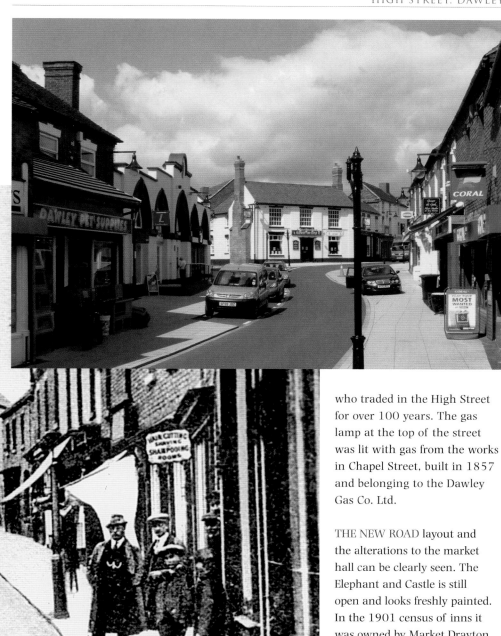

who traded in the High Street for over 100 years. The gas lamp at the top of the street was lit with gas from the works in Chapel Street, built in 1857 and belonging to the Dawley Gas Co. Ltd.

THE NEW ROAD layout and the alterations to the market hall can be clearly seen. The Elephant and Castle is still open and looks freshly painted. In the 1901 census of inns it was owned by Market Drayton Brewery Co. and had ten rooms on each floor and stabling for seven horses. It was mainly frequented by men from the mining industry. The road to the right of the inn is Burton Street.

WESLEYAN CHAPEL, DAWLEY

THE WESLEYAN CHAPEL, Dawley, *c.*1965. The chapel stood on the corner of High Street and Chapel Street. The building was erected in 1860 on the site of an earlier chapel built in 1819. The new chapel was a fine example of Victorian polychrome brickwork that was very fashionable at this time. Over 100 years ago the Revd William Stephenson Bestall was superintendent of the Dawley circuit, created in 1870, and the Revd William Hambley was minister.

IN THE 1960s several smaller chapels merged with the Dawley church. The new institution became known as the Central Methodist church and was the hub of Methodist work in the area. The ground floor of the chapel was converted into an interdenominational pastoral centre in 1967; the chapel was demolished in 1977. It was replaced by the building at the rear of the newly formed square and is known as the Dawley Christian Centre. The ornamental bandstand has seating in it for weary shoppers.

HIGH STREET, DAWLEY

HIGH STREET, DAWLEY, 25 April 1967. This photograph records the chaos caused by road works when the High Street was dug up to remake the road. The *Shropshire Star* headline read, 'This is Dawley High Street Today – A Hole In The Road To Beat Them All'. The County Council had set a four-week target for completion. This photograph was taken two weeks into the work and shows

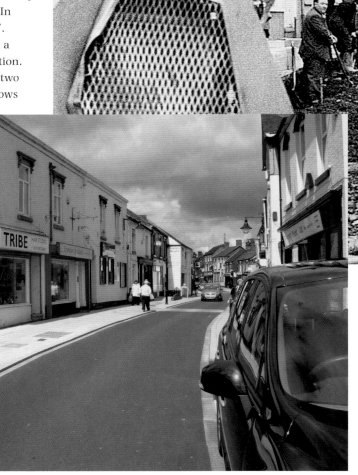

they were already off schedule. We are looking up the street towards the Elephant and Castle. The building jutting out on the left is Bailey's butchers shop.

THE NEW ROAD layout looks superb and hopefully will last for many years as the locals have been subjected to the inconvenience of three major road works in the High Street in the last forty-five years. Most of the buildings remain the same – although the ones on the left, next to Tribe, have been removed. The butcher's shop is still trading under the name of Dawley Meats.

HIGH STREET, DAWLEY

THE HIGH STREET, Dawley, *c.*1950. In *Bagshaw's Directory* for 1851 the population of Dawley is given as 8,641, with Dawley Green, on which the High Street was built, being the most densely populated part of the parish. The High Street at that time contained many good houses and shops in a variety of retail trades. The bungalow and petrol pump belonged to Joseph Poole, who owned a large garage just to the right of the monument. He also ran a bus service between Dawley and Wellington. The bus was known locally as the Heather Bell.

Unfortunately, however, the bus service stopped when a larger firm began running the same service at the same time but at a cheaper fare.

THE BUNGALOW AND garage were replaced by two modern shops and a branch of Barclays Bank, which opened on 12 August 1960. The memorial is to Dawley-born Captain Matthew Webb, who became the first man to swim the Channel in August 1875. He died on 24 July 1883 while attempting to swim the rapids at the foot of the Niagara Falls. The memorial has been moved several times but now seems to be back close to its original site. Inscribed on the monument are Webb's own words, 'Nothing great is easy'.

MORTON COPPICE, HORSEHAY

MORTON COPPICE, HORSEHAY, *c.*1900. A Horsehay resident is seen here with his donkey and cart, near Morton Coppice. Transport like this would have been a familiar sight around the villages and smaller towns in Shropshire, as they would often deliver necessary household items

and other goods around the area. In the background is the Primitive Methodist Chapel, erected in 1858 and built out of blue and yellow bricks. It served the people from Horsehay Potteries, Woodhouse Lane, Stoney Hill and Coalmoor in Little Wenlock.

THE CONGREGATION WERE joined by the members of the Wesleyan Chapel in Spring Gardens in 1968 and the chapel is still open for worship. A new road linking the Ironbridge by-pass to Heath Hill runs along the line of the old road. The spot where the donkey and cart once stood has been built on, and some bungalows now occupy the site. The upgraded road is a main link to the M54 motorway and the Princess Royal Hospital. The name of the village is old and is believed to have originated from the Anglo-Saxon name meaning 'a clearing in the forest where horses are kept'.

ST LUKE'S ROAD, DOSELEY

ST LUKE'S ROAD, Doseley, c.1925. The village is in the ecclesiastical parish of Dawley Parva. The houses are Victorian and date from about 1860. They back onto the railway – note the signal behind the second house from the left. The church of St Luke from which the road takes its name was erected in 1844 but was made redundant in about 1980 and was converted

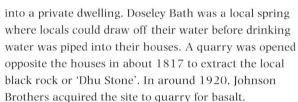

into a private dwelling. Doseley Bath was a local spring where locals could draw off their water before drinking water was piped into their houses. A quarry was opened opposite the houses in about 1817 to extract the local black rock or 'Dhu Stone'. In around 1920, Johnson Brothers acquired the site to quarry for basalt.

THE VILLAGE IS very rural and it is hard to believe it is in the middle of a large new town. The houses still stand but are hidden by trees and bushes used to landscape the bank. Some of the houses have also erected garages near the road. The quarry has now closed but residents are worried about plans to build houses on the site and the impact it will have on the community.

HOLYWELL LANE, LITTLE DAWLEY

HOLYWELL LANE, LITTLE Dawley, *c.*1930. The photographer has his back to Gravel Leasowes and is looking up the lane towards The Stocking, probably named after Stocking Farm. These were squatters' cottages, some dating back to the 1770s, on land belonging to the Earl of Craven. They were small and unsanitary, with some having upper floors built over the ground floors of other properties.

THE COTTAGES WERE demolished in the 1970s, removing families who had occupied the houses for several generations. Note the remains of the building on the right, just visible under the undergrowth. The lane remains unadopted although there are a number of houses there. The setting is tranquil and the only sound to be heard is birds singing.

THE CENOTAPH, MADELEY

THE CENOTAPH, MADELEY, *c.*1935. The history of the town dates back to Saxon times.
In the thirteenth century the manor belonged to Wenlock Abbey, who extended the town
by clearing more woodland. The Cenotaph stood at the junction of Park Street and Church
Street until 3 June 1970, when it was re-sited in Russell Square, by the new shopping centre.
It was always considered a traffic hazard and on Armistice Day the parade would completely
block the road for the duration of the service.

A NEW TESCO store now dominates the centre of the view and a mini island has replaced the war memorial, opening up the junction and making it safer for traffic. The memorial now stands around 60 yards away from its original site, in an open area behind the trees on the left (behind the library and to the side of the Anstice Hall).

THE ANSTICE MEMORIAL INSTITUTE, MADELEY

THE ANSTICE MEMORIAL Institute, Madeley, c.1910. The institute was built in 1869 in memory of John Anstice, an ironmaster who had died two years earlier. It was designed by John Johnson of London in the Italianate style, cost about £3,000 and is reputed to be the first working men's club in the world. Its accommodation included a lecture hall that seated 750, a billiard room, a smoking room and a reading room and library that contained over 2,000 volumes. The library closed in 1942. The hall was also used for social events, dances

and theatre. In October 1945 the Craft Hermits Repertory Company presented J.B. Priestley's *Dangerous Corners* at the invitation of the Madeley Joint Hospitals' Appeal Fund Committee.

DURING THE REDEVELOPMENT of the 1960s a new pedestrianized shopping complex was built around it. Recently that development has been replaced, and a new road now allows traffic through the area. The building on the left is Madeley Library, once inside the hall. The hall is still used for plays, dances and other social events.

LINCOLN HILL

THE IRONWORKS, COALBROOKDALE, *c.* 1920. This photograph was taken from Lincoln Hill looking north-west towards the Wrekin, with Jigger's Bank towards the top right. The building in the centre with the clock tower is the Great Warehouse. The Revd Mr Richard Warner described

the valley in 1801 as, 'hemmed in by high rocky banks, finely wooded,' that 'would be exceedingly picturesque, were it not for the huge foundries, which, volcano like, send up volumes of smoke into the air.' The company became famous for its ornamental cast-iron work, a reputation greatly enhanced by its display at the Great Exhibition of 1851, with such exhibits as 'The Boy and Swan Fountain'.

IN THE PAST 100 years the side of Lincoln Hill has become densely wooded and it is virtually impossible to get a clear shot of the works. This view was taken from a pathway between the Rotunda and Lincoln Hill. Many of the buildings have changed and the large chimneys have been demolished. The clock tower on the top of the Great Warehouse is still visible. It is dated 1843 and was added five years after the warehouse was built. The Great Warehouse is now the Coalbrookdale Museum of Iron.

COALBROOKDALE STATION

COALBROOKDALE STATION, *c.*1910. The station was situated just south of the Coalbrookdale ironworks and at the beginning of the nineteenth century was an extremely busy area. Trains going south from the station passed through Buildwas Junction and Farley Halt to Much Wenlock. In 1905 the stationmaster was William Marshall and the goods manager was William Prue. The buildings and platforms were very substantial and typical examples of GWR architecture.The station closed to passenger traffic on 23 July 1962 and to freight on 6 July 1964.

ALTHOUGH OFFICIALLY CLOSED, part of the line remains and is used by trains to transport coal across the Severn to Buildwas power station. The platform and buildings on the right have been removed but the main station building on the left remains. The station and the surrounding land is known as the Green Wood Centre and used by Small Woods Association, 'who work to achieve sustainably managed woods across the UK, delivering benefits to society for landscape, wildlife and people and supporting a thriving woodland economy.'

IRONBRIDGE FROM BENTHALL EDGE

IRONBRIDGE, c.1900. The town of Ironbridge takes its name from the bridge that was erected in 1779 and caused the growth of the town, perched on the steep limestone cliff overlooking the Severn Gorge. St Luke's was consecrated in 1837. To mark the occasion, James Thompson of the Lightmoor Works presented the church with a silver communion service. The new church was able to accommodate 1,062 people and from the beginning attracted large congregations. On Census Sunday in 1851 the morning service attracted 500 adults and 80 children, and at evensong the congregation was 700. The church was designed by Thomas Smith of Madeley.

THIS VIEW IS taken from Bridge Bank, which leads to Broseley. Many of the buildings on this side of the river have been demolished, opening up a better view of the bridge in the centre. The buildings on the opposite bank have also been removed but beyond that very little has changed: St Luke's church still stands proudly on the hill, and, below, the market hall and the Tontine Inn are still open for business. The area above the church known as Hodge Bower has also altered very little, although some of the buildings are now obscured by trees.

IRONBRIDGE AND BROSELEY STATION

IRONBRIDGE AND BROSELEY Station, *c.*1905. The station was on the Severn Valley line, which was called the 'Holiday Run' by the drivers because of its beautiful scenery. The line was operated by GWR and the station stood between Buildwas and Coalport Stations. The photograph gives a good view of the footbridge and the level-crossing gates, operated from the signal box on

the left. The engine is heading towards Shrewsbury and is a GWR 0-6-0 tender engine. There was genuine sadness when the line closed on 7 September 1963 and a large crowd of railway enthusiasts gathered to watch the last train depart for Shrewsbury. The driver of that last train was Hugh Bell; the fireman was Michael Medlicott and the guard was Jack Madeley, all from Shrewsbury.

THIS IS THE junction of Bridge Bank and Ladywood. The old bridge is just to the left of the view and the river just beyond the cars. The station and the surrounding buildings have all been removed and the area is now a car park. However, a section of railway track is just visible on the road leading in to the car park to indicate its original route.

THE MARKET PLACE, IRONBRIDGE

THE MARKET PLACE, Ironbridge, *c*.1900. The Friday market was started about 1800. The Market Hall on the left originally had an open arcaded ground floor, with two upper storeys and an attic. The open ground floor had been filled in with shops by 1847. Mrs Bartlett of Marnwood House erected the red granite drinking fountain in 1862, in memory of her husband, the Revd John Bartlett, the vicar of Buildwas from 1822 until 1861 and a man who took great interest in local affairs.

WHEN THE ROAD in front of the market place was altered, the memorial was removed and hidden way above the Waterloo Street car park. The Ironbridge Pharmacy is in the old Butter Market, which also had an open potato market at the rear. Like the Market Hall, the open ground floor was filled in to form a shop. The dispensing chemists Bates and Hunt, who had other shops in the area, opened a store there in the 1920s. They were also agricultural chemists, photographic suppliers and wine and spirit merchants.

LIMESTONE PIT, IRONBRIDGE

LIMESTONE PIT, IRONBRIDGE, c.1890. This is one of the limestone pits near the top of Lincoln Hill. Limestone has been mined and quarried from this area for hundreds of years, and as early as 1647 it was recorded that three men were killed at the limekilns there. By 1795 Richard Reynolds was in control of the mines but ownership later passed to the Madeley Wood Co. Work stopped for a short while in the nineteenth century and large-scale mining and quarrying never took place there again. The Madeley Wood Co. employed three men to work it in 1892, but by 1902 the mine was owned by John Hill, who worked it with one other man until it closed in 1907.

THE NAME LINCOLN Hill is thought to derive from 'Limekiln Hill'. The photographer is standing on the corner of Hodge Bower with Church Hill on the left, looking down Lincoln Hill towards the Gorge and Benthall Edge. The house on the junction is called Rock House; note the small service hatch in the wall on both views. The mine area has been reclaimed by nature and the gas lamp replaced by an electric light.

THE COALPORT AND JACKFIELD MEMORIAL BRIDGE

THE COALPORT AND Jackfield Memorial Bridge, 1922. Crowds of onlookers line the banks of the Severn for the opening of the new footbridge. It acted as a memorial to the twenty-four servicemen from both communities who had sacrificed their lives during the First World War.

A plaque on the bridge has the following epitaph, 'THIS BRIDGE IS FREE, O TREAD IT REVERENTLY, IN MEMORY OF THOSE WHO DIED FOR THEE'. The bridge replaced an old ferry that took people across at the same point.

THE COUNTY COUNCIL took responsibility for the bridge in 1979, when it was partially restored. Towards the end of the 1990s it was considered unsafe and there was considerable speculation about its future. Thankfully, however, in 2000 – at a cost of £430,000 – it was dismantled and transported to Wrexham, where it was restored before being put back *in situ*. The project was funded by Telford-based Onyx Environmental Trust, a grant from the Heritage Lottery Fund and the Telford and Wrekin Council. Note that the new approach has been put at an angle for safety reasons.

THE HAY INCLINED PLANE

THE HAY INCLINED Plane, *c.*1900. By using the Hay Inclined Plane, canal boats could be raised and lowered between the Shropshire Canal and the basin at Coalport, on the banks of the River Severn. The tub boats were floated on to wheeled cradles that carried them on the iron rails. On the right, at the top of the incline, is the engine house. The steam engine was used to pull the cradles and boats out of the water and to help pull heavier loads up the hill.

The height of the incline was 207ft, and it was possible to deliver a pair of 6-ton boats from one level to the other in three and a half minutes, compared with the four hours needed with an ordinary lock system.

THE HAY INCLINED Plane is now part of the Blists Hill Open Air Museum. The engine house and part of the Shropshire Union Canal at the top are now obscured by trees. A small section of canal at the bottom also survives, which has a towpath that links the plane to the Coalport China Museum. The plane was named after Hay Farm that stood close by, which was once the home of John Rose, the owner of the china works.

HIGH STREET, COALPORT

HIGH STREET, COALPORT, *c*.1910.
William Reynolds laid out plans for
Coalport in about 1793 as a port where
goods could be interchanged between
the River Severn and the local canal
system. It was intended to become a
major port to bring in all the necessary
imports and to ship out all the locally
made items. Warehouses were built
to hold all the merchandise and new
industries opened, including a soap
factory, a chain and rope works and
the world-famous china works that was
founded in 1796.

THE MAIN DIFFERENCES between the
old and new images are that the tall
buildings at the end of the road have

been demolished, the house in the centre of the row has been lowered and the road has been raised, leaving the houses in a dip. The men at the end of the row are standing outside the Brewery Inn. The proprietor of the inn is Roger Hotchkiss, who is the longest-serving landlord in Shropshire. Accommodation at the inn offers bed and breakfast, a riverside holiday cottage and River Severn fishing.

COALPORT BRIDGE

COALPORT BRIDGE, *c*.1920. The first bridge was constructed entirely of wood and opened in 1780. It was known as Preen's Eddy Bridge, designed by William Haywood and built by Robert Palmer. After it was severely damaged by the great flood of 1795, it was converted into a single-span wooden bridge over three iron ribs. The bridge we know today was constructed in 1818 by John Onions. After the centre rib of the old bridge was fractured, he converted it into an all-iron bridge with five ribs.

IN RECENT YEARS the bridge has been put under a great deal of strain as it is still open to traffic. In the autumn of 2005 it was closed for several weeks and around £1 million was spent on strengthening the structure. A height limit and speed restriction have also been implemented. Behind the nearest house on the far right was Coalport East Station, which was the terminus of a branch line from Wellington. The houses on the bank are still there but obscured by trees. The one on the right is now called Shangri-La; the one in the centre is called Ferndale, and the one on the left the Old Coach House.

If you enjoyed this book, you may also be interested in...

Haunted Telford

PHILIP SOLOMON

Telford plays host to many spirits from the past. The surrounding areas of Ironbridge Gorge and Coalbrookdale are haunted by numerous ghostly apparitions that appear to date from the time of the Industrial Revolution. From heart-stopping accounts of ghosts, manifestations and related supernatural phenomena to first-hand encounters with spirits, this collection of stories contains both new and well-known spooky stories from in and around Telford.

978 0 7524 5766 6

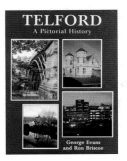

Telford: A Pictorial History

GEORGE EVANS & RON BRISCOE

Telford may be a new town, but it also contains a World Heritage Site as well as the famous Ironbridge Gorge Museum. It is an area renowned for pioneering and innovations, from Darby's furnace and the first railway engine to the discovery of digitalis and the invention of electric propulsion.

978 0 8503 3955 0

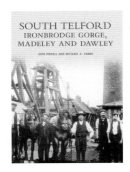

South Telford, Ironbridge Gorge, Madeley & Dawley

JOHN POWELL & MICHAEL VANNS

In the eighteenth and nineteenth centuries, the Ironbridge Gorge was the scene of dramatic industrial activity which today's resident or visitor would find difficult to envisage. However, it was the rapid growth of the iron industry which transformed this part of East Shropshire. The old-established town of Madeley expanded to meet the needs of a growing workforce, whilst Dawley developed as an important centre for mining and iron making. The town of Ironbridge sprang up as a direct result of the building of the Iron Bridge, and another settlement was created at Coalport. On the south side of the river, Jackfield thrived as a busy inland port. From the mid-nineteenth century, problems with transport and the availability of better raw materials elsewhere led to the migration of the iron-making industry to other parts of the country. Thus, by the time photography came on the scene, the area, although still dependent on heavy industry, was in decline. This trend continued into the twentieth century and was only reversed with the arrival of Telford New Town in the 1960s.

978 0 7524 0125 6

Visit our website and discover thousands of other History Press books.

www.thehistorypress.co.uk